NATIONAL GEOGRAPHIC

MW01539014

Shaggy

Beatrice Duggan

We take Shaggy to the dog groomer.

Super Premium Pet Foods
"Try us for a week.....Your Pet Will Love Us For Life"
AVAILABLE HERE

She brushes Shaggy.

She trims Shaggy.

She washes Shaggy.

She dries Shaggy.

Look at Shaggy now!